Present over Perfect

Present over Perfect

Inspiration for Mindful Moments

CICO BOOKS

Published in 2026 by CICO Books
An imprint of Ryland Peters & Small Ltd
20–21 Jockey's Fields 1452 Davis Bugg Road
London WC1R 4BW Warrenton, NC 27589
www.rylandpeters.com
Email: euregulations@rylandpeters.com

10 9 8 7 6 5 4 3 2 1

Photography credits can be found on page 144

A CIP record for this book is available from the British Library.
US Library of Congress CIP data has been applied for.

ISBN: 978-1-80065-580-5

Printed in China

Designer: Geoff Borin
Commissioning editor: Kristine Pidkameny
Assistant editor: Danielle Rawlings
Senior designer: Emily Breen
Art director: Sally Powell
Creative director: Leslie Harrington
Head of production: Patricia Harrington
Publishing manager: Carmel Edmonds

The authorised representative in the EEA is
Authorised Rep Compliance Ltd.,
Ground Floor. 71 Lower Baggot Street,
Dublin, D01 P593, Ireland
www.arccompliance.com

FSC
www.fsc.org
MIX
Paper | Supporting responsible forestry
FSC® C106563

Introduction

In the rush of our daily lives—punctuated by endless to-do lists and digital distractions—it's easy to forget the simple yet profound power of being present. Mindfulness is not a destination but a gentle returning, again and again, to the here and now. It is the practice of noticing life as it unfolds, without judgment, and with full awareness of each moment.

This book is a curated collection of quotes that capture the essence of mindfulness. Drawn from a wide range of voices—such as famous playwright William Shakespeare, French missionary Thérèse of Lisieux, poet Emily Dickinson, and writer Mark Twain—each quote offers a moment of pause, a window into presence, and a quiet invitation to return to yourself. Some words will comfort, some will challenge, and others may awaken something deep within you. All are chosen to serve as touchstones for reflection, clarity, and peace.

You don't need to read this book from cover to cover. Open it at random, linger on a page, or carry a quote with you throughout your day. Let these words be gentle reminders that life is happening now—not in the past we cannot change, nor in the future we cannot predict, but in this moment, right here.

"IT IS NEVER TOO LATE TO LEARN WHAT IS ALWAYS NECESSARY TO KNOW."

SENECA

Embrace the
wonder of now

"THERE IS NOTHING EITHER GOOD OR BAD,
BUT THINKING MAKES IT SO."

WILLIAM SHAKESPEARE

"GIVE EVERY DAY THE CHANCE

TO BECOME THE MOST

BEAUTIFUL DAY OF YOUR LIFE."

MARK TWAIN

Make it matter

I am focused
yet relaxed

"Yesterday I was clever, so I wanted to change the world. Today I am wise, so I am changing myself."

RUMI

I am willing to change

"THE SMALLEST ACT OF KINDNESS IS WORTH MORE THAN THE GREATEST INTENTION."

KAHLIL GIBRAN

"THE BEST THING ONE CAN DO WHEN IT'S RAINING IS TO LET IT RAIN."

HENRY WADSWORTH LONGFELLOW

"WHAT LIES BEHIND YOU AND WHAT LIES IN FRONT OF YOU,

PALES IN COMPARISON TO WHAT LIES INSIDE OF YOU."

RALPH WALDO EMERSON

Pause, breathe, rest

Be true to yourself

“IT’S AMAZING HOW LOVELY COMMON THINGS BECOME, IF ONE ONLY KNOWS HOW TO LOOK AT THEM.”

LOUISA MAY ALCOTT

Cultivate compassion

“It isn’t what we say or think that defines us, but what we do.”

JANE AUSTEN

Find purpose and joy

"WE ARE THE WORDS;

WE ARE THE MUSIC;

WE ARE THE THING ITSELF."

VIRGINIA WOOLF

Tune in to
your body

"Give yourself a gift:
the present moment."

MARCUS AURELIUS

I am here, I am now

WHEN I LET GO OF WHAT I AM,
I BECOME WHAT I MIGHT BE.

LAO TZU

It begins with you

Listen to the whispers around you

"Peace is always beautiful."

WALT WHITMAN

"WHEN WE YIELD TO DISCOURAGEMENT IT IS USUALLY BECAUSE WE GIVE

TOO MUCH THOUGHT TO THE PAST AND TO THE FUTURE."

THÉRÈSE OF LISIEUX

Kindness grows

"Forever is composed of nows."

EMILY DICKINSON

"LIFE CAN ONLY TAKE PLACE IN THE PRESENT MOMENT. IF WE LOSE THE PRESENT MOMENT, WE LOSE LIFE."

BUDDHA

Rest is recovery

"THE MOST IMPORTANT THING IN LIFE IS TO STOP SAYING 'I WISH' AND START SAYING 'I WILL.' CONSIDER NOTHING IMPOSSIBLE, THEN TREAT POSSIBILITIES AS PROBABILITIES."

CHARLES DICKENS

Cultivate clarity

"THE PAST, THE PRESENT, AND THE FUTURE ARE REALLY ONE: THEY ARE TODAY."

HARRIET BEECHER STOWE

"The important work of moving the world forward does not wait to be done by perfect men."

GEORGE ELIOT

Seize the day

Travel light

"It takes a great deal of courage to see the world in all its tainted glory, and still to love it."

OSCAR WILDE

Be patient

"IT IS BETTER TO HAVE DREAMED
A THOUSAND DREAMS THAT NEVER WERE
THAN NEVER TO HAVE DREAMED AT ALL."

ALEXANDER PUSHKIN

Catch the kindness...

here, there, everywhere

Moments awaken

"THE LIGHT CONSTANTLY CHANGES, AND THAT ALTERS THE ATMOSPHERE AND BEAUTY OF THINGS EVERY MINUTE."

CLAUDE MONET

“WE ARE SURROUNDED BY POETRY ON ALL SIDES.”

VINCENT VAN GOGH

"Time stays long enough for anyone who will use it."

LEONARDO DA VINCI

Give yourself the gift of right now

Find the glimmers

"IN STILLNESS, THE MUDDIED WATER RETURNS TO CLARITY."

LAOZI

Allow and let
it all be

"THERE EXISTS ONLY THE PRESENT INSTANT... A NOW WHICH ALWAYS AND WITHOUT END IS ITSELF NEW. THERE IS NO YESTERDAY

NOR ANY TOMORROW, BUT ONLY NOW, AS IT WAS A THOUSAND YEARS AGO AND AS IT WILL BE A THOUSAND YEARS HENCE."

MEISTER ECKHART

I choose peace

"EVERYWHERE IS HERE
AND EVERY WHEN IS NOW."

DANTE ALIGHIERI

Presence
is essence

Create your own magic

"TO SEE A WORLD IN A GRAIN OF SAND AND A HEAVEN IN A WILDFLOWER."

WILLIAM BLAKE

“Now’s the day and now’s the hour.”

ROBERT BURNS

Be a living meditation

"THE BEGINNING IS ALWAYS TODAY."

MARY SHELLEY

Let go of self-judgment

"BE THOU THE RAINBOW IN THE STORMS OF LIFE. THE EVENING BEAM THAT SMILES THE CLOUDS AWAY, AND TINTS TOMORROW WITH PROPHETIC RAY."

LORD BYRON

Choose to pay attention

"My destination is no longer a place, rather a new way of seeing."

MARCEL PROUST

With each breath
I clear my mind

"WHAT IS DELAYED IS NOT LOST."

JULIETTE DROUET

"IT IS ONLY THROUGH SHADOWS THAT ONE COMES TO KNOW THE LIGHT."

SAINT CATHERINE OF SIENA

Rest in the present

"EVERY PART OF THE JOURNEY IS OF IMPORTANCE TO THE WHOLE."

TERESA OF ÁVILA

I respond rather than react

“PATIENCE IS ALSO A FORM OF ACTION.”

AUGUSTE RODIN

"WHAT I DO NOT SEE, I DO NOT KNOW. I SEE, HEAR, AND KNOW SIMULTANEOUSLY AND

LEARN WHAT I KNOW AS IF IN A MOMENT."

HILDEGARD OF BINGEN

Create value: be present

"Let us accept truth,
even when it surprises us
and alters our views."

GEORGE SAND

Remember to breathe

"Anything you can imagine you can make real."

JULES VERNE

Live with kindness

“Every day is a journey,
and the journey itself
is home.”

MATSUO BASHŌ

"JUDGE EACH DAY NOT BY THE HARVEST YOU REAP BUT BY THE SEEDS YOU PLANT."

WILLIAM ARTHUR WARD

Make a connection
It's never too late
to be present

"WE SEE THE BRIGHTNESS
OF A NEW PAGE WHERE EVERYTHING
YET CAN HAPPEN."

RAINER MARIA RILKE

Savor the journey

"WE MAY MAKE OUR FUTURE BY THE BEST USE

OF THE PRESENT. THERE IS NO MOMENT LIKE THE PRESENT."

MARIA EDGEWORTH

“If I don’t enjoy myself now, when shall I?”

OMAR KHAYYAM

Each day is an

opportunity for renewal

"FOR ME, THE GREATEST BEAUTY ALWAYS LIES IN THE GREATEST CLARITY."

GOTTHOLD EPHRAIM LESSING

"Lose not yourself in a far-off time; seize the moment that is thine."

FRIEDRICH SCHILLER

Attune to a new way of being

"When you play, never mind who listens to you."

ROBERT SCHUMANN

"WHY HURRY OVER BEAUTIFUL THINGS? WHY NOT LINGER AND ENJOY THEM?"

CLARA SCHUMANN

Allow the moment to unfold

"LIFE IS THE SPACE BETWEEN OUR THINGS."

CLAUDE DEBUSSY

"In difficult times, carry something beautiful in your heart."

BLAISE PASCAL

“It is absurd to look for perfection.”

CAMILLE PISSARRO

Clear mind, quiet heart

"HAPPINESS IS RIGHT IN FRONT OF YOU."

HAFEZ

"SOMETIMES, THE MOST PROFOUND OF AWAKENINGS COME WRAPPED IN THE QUIETEST OF MOMENTS."

STEPHEN CRANE

Permit a sacred pause

Perfection is an illusion

"SILENCE MORE MUSICAL THAN ANY SONG."

CHRISTINA ROSSETTI

"YOUR EYES SMILE PEACE."

DANTE GABRIEL ROSSETTI

"Life's a voyage that's homeward bound."

HERMAN MELVILLE

You are enough

"THE PRESENT MOMENT
IS A POWERFUL GODDESS."

JOHANN WOLFGANG VON GOETHE

ALICE:

"This is impossible."

THE MAD HATTER:

"Only if you believe it is."

LEWIS CARROLL

“BEHOLD THIS DAY.
IT IS YOURS TO MAKE.”

BLACK ELK

Life is moving through you

"We carry the seeds of happiness with us wherever we go."

MARTHA WASHINGTON

"What you are looking for is what is looking."

SAINT FRANCIS OF ASSISI

Come home to the present moment

Picture credits

© Adobestock.com and the following creators:
ADDICTIVE STOCK: pages 1, 2–3, 5, 6–7, 16, 26, 35, 40, 53, 64, 79, 84, 90, 99, 107, 120, 125, 139, 144; **Juliaap:** pages 8–9; **Sumon:** pages 10–11, 28–29, 48–49, 58–59, 70–71, 88–89, 102–103, 110–111, 122–123, 134–135; **PixelArtBox:** pages 12, 14, 15, 18, 19, 20, 21, 23, 24, 25, 36, 37, 38, 39, 42, 43, 54, 55, 60, 61, 62, 63, 68, 69, 72, 75, 80, 82, 83, 87, 92, 93, 94, 108, 109, 116, 117, 119, 128, 129, 133, 136, 137, 140, 142, 143; **Kaz:** pages 13, 32–33, 46–47, 76–77, 96–97, 114–115, 130–131; **Chalabala:** page 18–19; **margakarya:** pages 22, 44–45, 56–57, 73; **oatawa:** pages 24–25; **YURII Seleznov:** pages 30–31; **Richie Chan:** pages 42–43; **Judit:** pages 50–51; **Lou W/peopleimages.com:** pages 54–55; **Juan:** pages 60–61; **Pixel-Shot:** pages 66–67; **Juancat:** pages 74–75; **Николай Алибабаевич:** pages 80–81; **New Africa:** pages 86–87; **Aleksandra:** pages 94–95; **Maryana:** pages 100–101; **trofalena:** pages 104–105; **Choat:** pages 112–113; **astrosystem:** pages 118–119; **kieferpix:** pages 126–127; **DavidPrado:** pages 140–141